Discovering Mission San Luis Obispo de Tolosa

BY JEANNETTE BUCKLEY

Cavendish
Square
New York

Published in 2015 by Cavendish Square Publishing, LLC
243 5th Avenue, Suite 136, New York, NY 10016

CPSIA Compliance Information: Batch #WS14CSQ

All websites were available and accurate when this book was sent to press.

Buckley, Jeannette.
Discovering Mission San Luis Obispo de Tolosa / Jeannette Buckley.
pages cm. — (California missions)
Includes index.
ISBN 978-1-62713-091-2 (hardcover) ISBN 978-1-62713-093-6 (ebook)
1. Mission San Luis Obispo de Tolosa (San Luis Obispo, Calif.)—History—Juvenile literature. 2. Spanish mission buildings—California—San Luis Obispo—History—Juvenile literature. 3. Franciscans—California—San Luis Obispo—History—Juvenile literature. 4. Chumash Indians—Missions—California—San Luis Obispo—History—Juvenile literature. 5. California—History—To 1846—Juvenile literature. I. Title.

F869.M665B83 2015
979.4'78—dc23

2014006944

Library of Congress Cataloging-in-Publication Data

Editorial Director: Dean Miller
Editor: Kristen Susienka
Copy Editor: Cynthia Roby
Art Director: Jeffrey Talbot
Designer: Douglas Brooks
Photo Researcher: J8 Media
Production Manager: Jennifer Ryder-Talbot
Production Editor: David McNamara

The photographs in this book are used by permission and through the courtesy of: Cover photo by Glow Images, Inc/Glow/Getty Images; Rennett Stowe/File:Mission San Luis Obispo.jpg/Wikimedia Commons, 1; Barry Winiker/Stockbyte/Getty Images, 4; Daderot/File:Basketry tray, Chumash, Santa Barbara Mission, early 1800s - Native American collection - Peabody Museum, Harvard University - DSC05558.JPG/Wikimedia Commons, 8; Michael "Mike" L. Baird/File:Pictographs on Painted Rock.jpg/Wikimedia Commons, 10; Pentacle Press, 12; © 2014 Pentacle Press, 13; SaltyBoatr/File:Gaspar de Portola statue.jpg/Wikimedia Commons, 14; John E Marriott/All Canada Photos/Getty Images, 16; Steve Heap/Shutterstock.com, 17; © North Wind Picture Archives/Alamy, 19; Courtesy of Monterey County Free Libraries, 21; File:San Luis Obispo de Tolozo LACMA M.79.53.12.jpg/Wikimedia Commons, 22; © North Wind/North Wind Picture Archives, 26; BSIP/UIG/Getty Images, 29; Courtesy CMRC, 30; INAH/File:Generales del Trigarante.jpg/Wikimedia Commons, 32; File:Pio Pico.jpg/Wikimedia Commons, 33; Stringer/Archive Photos/Getty Images, 34; Hemis.fr/SuperStock, 36; Glow Images, Inc/Glow/Getty Images, 41.

Printed in the United States of America

Mission San Luis Obispo de Tolosa is one of the only missions still in its original location.

1
The Spanish Explore Alta California

San Luis Obispo is a typical California community, filled with businesses, houses, and families. The city is also home to an historical landmark, the remains of Mission San Luis Obispo de Tolosa. People can still visit the church, built from whitewashed **adobe** brick, complete with a red tiled roof and its three original bells hanging over the entrance. The **mission**, one of twenty-one built centuries ago throughout California by the Spanish friars (called *frays* in Spanish), fundamentally changed the lives of the Native people of the area.

SPANISH EXPLORERS ARRIVE IN THE NEW WORLD

The Spanish interest in the land we now know as California began more than 500 years ago. After Christopher Columbus sailed to the lands that Europeans called the New World (North America, South America, and Central America) in the late 1400s, the king of Spain sent explorers to learn more about the discovery. In the 1500s, the Spanish sailed to California in search of gold, spices, and other riches.

Wealth was not the only reason Spain wanted to claim the New World. The Spanish practiced **Catholicism**, a branch of Christianity, and believed that everyone should follow the teachings of Jesus Christ and the Bible. They wanted to **convert** the Native people in the region to Christianity because they believed that only **Christians** went to heaven after death.

The Spanish sent Juan Rodríguez Cabrillo to explore the *Alta California* coast in 1542. He discovered the area that is now called San Diego Bay. Under Spanish rule, the name *Las Californias* described the part of Mexico that is now the Baja Peninsula and the land that is now the state of California. The southern section of Las Californias was called *Baja*, or "lower," California, while the northern section was called Alta, or "upper," California. Alta California eventually became the state of California.

Over the next two centuries Alta California was explored little because there were no riches or a direct water route from Europe to Asia, which is what Spain had hoped to find in America. The Spanish concentrated on settling Baja California, known as New Spain, and enlisted priests to run missions, or religious communities. These communities were successful, and in 1769 Spain's king, Carlos III, decided to start missions in Alta California, to be run by Franciscan priests. At this time Spain was worried that other countries, such as England and Russia, would claim the land in that area before them. Setting up the mission system, however, would help ensure Spain's control over the land and the people.

2
The Chumash

The main Native tribe that lived near Mission San Luis Obispo de Tolosa was called the Obispeño Chumash, or Northern Chumash. A few Salinan tribes also lived in the area. The Chumash passed down their traditions and histories orally. They also left behind artifacts and belongings, such as shell ornaments and stone bowls, that historians and archaeologists have unearthed and pieced together to expand the history of these ancient people. Written accounts by Spanish explorers have also aided to the understanding of who the Chumash were and how they lived.

DWELLINGS

Like other California tribes, the Chumash lived in small villages near rivers, streams, and the ocean. Their houses, however, were larger than those of the other Native people. According to written accounts by the Spanish, the Chumash had what resembled beds, as well as rooms in their houses. Normally circular dwellings, the houses and roofs were made of tree branches and reeds called tule, which the Chumash tied together to hold the materials in place. Each home had a fire pit. A circular hole was cut into the roof for the smoke to exit. The houses were easily taken down if

The Chumash were expert basket makers. Their intricate designs were unique to their tribe, and many examples still exist today.

the tribe needed to leave the area to find more food. For that reason, some Chumash were also **nomadic**.

FOOD

The Chumash were hunters and gatherers, meaning they lived off the land and animals around them. The men did the hunting and fishing. They made tools and weapons from various objects found in their environment—animal bones, shells, and rocks—which they used to kill game such as deer, bear, rabbits, squirrels, and birds. They built canoes that were used to fish in the nearby rivers and bays. The Chumash women collected much of the family's food, such as insects, grass seeds, clams and shellfish, and wild cherries. They also cared for the children. Most of the food was collected in baskets made from reeds. Some of the baskets were lined with tar so they could hold water.

Acorns were an important source of nutrition for the Chumash because they could be easily stored and used to make many kinds of food. The Native people collected as many of the nuts as possible during the fall months. It was then that the Chumash moved to temporary shelters near forests of oak trees so they could collect the plants and nuts, and be protected from harsh winds. They remained there throughout the winter. The Chumash used specific lands and sometimes fought with other groups that tried to gather food or hunt in their area.

CLOTHING

The Chumash women used animal hides and tule for clothing. They made skirts from tule or strips of rabbit fur decorated with shells. In warm weather, both men and children wore little or no clothing. In cooler months, everyone wore animal furs for warmth. Both men and women wore their hair long. Sometimes the women decorated their hair with bands of shells.

The Chumash wore special accessories, such as beads, pendants, hair ornaments; and headdresses made of feathers, bone, stone, and shells during ceremonies. Some ceremony participants wore animal heads as hats and strung bear claws on a necklace. They often painted their bodies for **rituals** that included dancing and singing. The Chumash held ceremonies to acknowledge solstices—meaning seasonal changes—coming of age, marriages, births, and deaths.

RELIGIOUS BELIEFS AND PRACTICES

The Chumash people had religious beliefs based on the natural world around them. They had many gods, including ones based on the sun and moon. The Chumash believed these deities could do both good and bad, and tried to honor these gods with ceremonies and gifts. Their medicine men, also known as shamans, would use dancing and singing to eliminate the evil spirits that they believed caused sickness. The shamans also believed in the healing power of herbs.

Many Native tribes, including the Chumash, Salinan, and Yokut, sometimes marked special events by painting designs on the walls of caves.

3
The Mission System

The Missions of Alta California were not the first New World settlements built by the Spanish. As early as the 1500s, they sent friars, settlers, and soldiers to both Central and South America to build missions in those regions. The Spanish governed their colonies in New Spain from their capital, which they named Mexico City.

CONVERTING THE PEOPLE

The first religious settlements in the New World were built in areas where many Native people lived. The friars hoped that by being close to the people they could more quickly teach them to adopt the lifestyle of the Spanish. Based on their judgment of the way the Native people lived—they did not go to school or wear much clothing, painted their bodies, lived in simple homes, and were not Christians—the Spanish believed them to be inferior. The Spaniards felt that the Native people needed instruction, and that they were the best people to guide the tribes. The goal was to make them like the Spanish in every way: religion, language, and traditions.

At the missions, neophytes learned farming techniques from the friars, such as how to plow fields.

What the first European settlers did not understand, however, was that the Native American lifestyle was a different but equally valuable culture. Today we hold a greater appreciation for diversity in lifestyles and cultures. But during this time in history, there was little respect for difference. As a result, many Native American cultures suffered at the missions.

The mission system saw friars teaching the Native people about the Spanish ways, particularly farming and caring for livestock such as sheep or cattle. In addition to farming, the friars taught the Native people how to become skilled in trades such as carpentry, blacksmithing, weaving, and leather making. The friars also taught them about Christianity. Once a Native person converted, they were allowed to live at the mission and were called **neophytes**.

MISSIONS OF ALTA CALIFORNIA

The missions in Alta California followed the same model as the Baja California missions. They also had extra help in the form of soldiers, who journeyed with the friars to find the right location for the mission. The soldiers established *presidios*, or forts, to protect the land and the people who came to settle in nearby *pueblos*, or towns. The first mission in Alta California was San Diego de Alcalá, established in 1769 by Fray Junípero Serra. Between 1769 and 1823, twenty other missions followed.

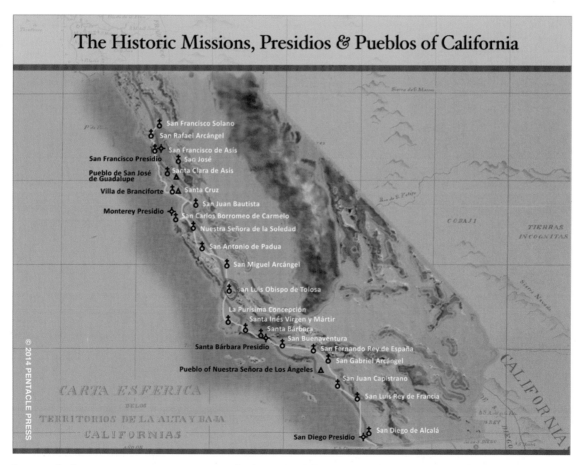

The Historic Missions, Presidios & Pueblos of California

San Francisco Solano
San Rafael Arcángel
San Francisco de Asís
San Francisco Presidio — San José
Pueblo de San José de Guadalupe — Santa Clara de Asís
Villa de Branciforte — Santa Cruz
San Juan Bautista
Monterey Presidio — San Carlos Borromeo de Carmelo
Nuestra Señora de la Soledad
San Antonio de Padua
San Miguel Arcángel
San Luis Obispo de Tolosa
La Purísima Concepción
Santa Inés Virgen y Mártir
Santa Bárbara
Santa Bárbara Presidio — San Buenaventura
San Fernando Rey de España
San Gabriel Arcángel
Pueblo of Nuestra Señora de Los Ángeles
San Juan Capistrano
San Luis Rey de Francia
San Diego Presidio — San Diego de Alcalá

CARTA ESFERICA
DE LOS
TERRITORIOS DE LA ALTA Y BAJA
CALIFORNIAS

CALIFORNIA

COBAJI

TIERRAS INCOGNITAS

In total, there were twenty-one missions and four presidios built along the coast. All were connected by a road called El Camino Real (indicated by the yellow line).

4
Founding the Mission

More than 200 men traveled north from New Spain to Alta California in order to launch the new mission system. The Spanish were worried about both English and Russian settlers disputing

Gaspár de Portolá was governor of Alta and Baja California from 1768 to 1770. He led an expedition to found the first Alta California mission.

the Spanish claim on the land. Two ports, San Diego and Monterey, were established by Captain Gaspár de Portolá, a nobleman by birth who was sent by Spain on an expedition to explore Alta California and claim new land. Portolá was also named governor of the Californias. Traveling with Portolá was Fray Junípero Serra, who would serve as the president of the missions. Since becoming a priest in 1737, Serra had been part of New Spain's mission system. The long, 750-mile (1,207-kilometer) journey to San Diego was difficult for the small, sickly Serra, as a previous insect (perhaps mosquito) bite had infected Serra's leg, causing it to swell painfully. Fray Serra refused to let his ailment stop him, even if others had to lift him onto a mule. This determination illustrated Serra's motto—"Always go forward. Never turn back."

PORTOLÁ'S EXPEDITION

Five expeditions—two by land and three by sea—departed New Spain. However, the third ship carrying supplies never arrived in San Diego and was later presumed lost at sea. Portolá's expeditions not only included soldiers, sailors, and friars, but also neophytes from the missions in New Spain. The Spanish hoped the neophytes could serve as translators. Only half of the group survived the journey. Some deserted, while others became ill with scurvy, a disease caused by a lack of fresh fruits and vegetables that contain vitamin C.

While Fray Serra founded Mission San Diego de Alcalá on July 16, 1769, Portolá departed with sixty-three men in search of Monterey. The Monterey area had been discovered in 1602 by Spanish explorer Sebastián Vizcaíno, who described it as "a rich land of great beauty with much promise as a seaport." Portolá's group searched for Vizcaíno's Monterey, but when they came across it, they did not recognize it. Tired and hungry, Portolá and his men decided to head back to San Diego. They were desperate for food when they entered the swampy valley surrounded by eroding hillsides. There they noticed that much of the soil was overturned and soon realized that grizzly bears had dug it up searching for roots to eat. One bear nearly killed them before they used their guns to slay it. Soon, more bears appeared and the group shot them and ate their meat. The Spanish called the land *el llano de los osos*, meaning "the Level of the Bears." It is also called *la cañada de los osos*, meaning "the Valley of the Bears."

Mission San Luis Obispo was founded in the Valley of the Bears in 1772.

A short time later, the Spanish found Monterey and established Mission San Carlos Borroméo del Río Carmelo. They also began a third settlement south of Monterey: the Mission San Antonio de Padua. These new missions were in their infancy and struggling to survive when they experienced a severe food shortage. An expedition of soldiers, led by the new military commander of New Spain, Pedro Fages, returned to the valley of the bears in 1772 to hunt. In three months, the group collected 9,000 pounds (4,082 kilograms) of meat, which saved the residents of Mission San Carlos Borroméo and Mission San Antonio from starvation. The expedition also traded with the Chumash for seeds and other foods. The Native people were fascinated by the guns used by the Spanish, as these weapons could kill grizzlies much easier than arrows. On occasion, the Chumash ate bear meat, but it was usually from cubs they had caught.

Fray Junípero Serra was the first leader of the Alta California mission system and founder of Mission San Luis Obispo de Tolosa.

FOUNDING MISSION SAN LUIS OBISPO DE TOLOSA

The Spanish thought that the area, which was rich with game and water and had a mild climate, would make a good site for a mission. They also found the Chumash to be friendly and helpful. On September 1, 1772, Fray Serra came to the Valley of the Bears and chose a spot for a new mission. Among the men who accompanied Serra was Pedro Fages. The men planted a cross in the ground near a stream. Fray Serra performed a Mass, or a Catholic Church service, and founded Mission San Luis Obispo de Tolosa. The mission was named for a beloved Franciscan friar, Saint Louis, a former prince who had left behind his claim to the throne and joined the order of priests. Fray Serra then left the mission in the care of Fray José Cavaller.

5
The Beginning of the Mission

After the founding ceremony at Mission San Luis Obispo in 1772, Fray Serra and others in the expedition needed to check on supplies at Mission San Diego de Alcalá. After this expedition left, only eight people—five soldiers, two neophytes, and Fray Cavaller—remained to begin building the mission. The group had brought three mules; some farming tools; food supplies such as sugar, flour, chocolate, and wheat; and some church items to be used at the mission. Two friars usually operated missions, but Cavaller was the only friar at Mission San Luis Obispo until 1798, when Fray Luis Antonio Martínez arrived.

BUILDING THE MISSION

In 1772, Fray Cavaller and the others at the mission were faced with many tasks. They needed to construct temporary shelters, including a church and living quarters. Tree boughs were cut and lashed together to form buildings. The people at the mission were thankful to receive help from the Chumash. In fact, they would not have survived their first year in Alta California without the hospitality of the Chumash.

The Chumash aided the Spanish at San Luis Obispo for several reasons. The two groups had established good relations by sharing food with each other in the past. The Chumash supplied seeds, while the Spanish offered bear meat. While most of the Chumash rejected gifts from the Spanish soldiers and friars, such as fabrics and tools, some agreed to help build the mission buildings. In return, the Spanish invited them to stay at the mission, and a few agreed and eventually became Christians. Attracting converts to the mission was slow in the early years, as the Chumash could obtain the food and materials they needed to survive without the help of the Spanish, and they were comfortable with their lifestyle. However, some Chumash were baptized. **Baptism** is a ceremony that is held when someone accepts the Christian faith.

At first, the Chumash lived independently from the mission. Over time, however, more Chumash people accepted Christianity and came to live at the missions.

The mission at San Luis Obispo followed the traditional quadrangle style of the other missions. This meant that the buildings formed a square shape. Each was constructed by soldiers and neophytes. In the early years of Mission San Luis Obispo de Tolosa, few neophytes lived there. This shortage of help slowed the construction process. The buildings were at first created out of wood, a material readily found around the area. The Spanish knew these structures were dangerous because they easily caught fire, though. They decided to reconstruct the buildings using adobe brick. The Spanish showed the Chumash how to make adobe from mud, straw, and water. Sometimes the workers used their feet to mix the materials, or they used animals to stomp it together. The adobe was then packed into wooden molds and the bricks were left to dry in the sun. Once the bricks hardened, they were ready to be used to form walls.

FIREPROOFING ROOFS AT THE MISSION

Like the initial mission buildings, the roofs were first constructed from simple materials, such as tule. However, in 1776, non-mission Natives attacked Mission San Luis Obispo. They set fire to one of the wooden roofs, which quickly spread to other buildings. Some of the living quarters, food supplies, tools, and other materials were destroyed. The Native people who attacked the mission believed that the Spanish were trespassing on their land and changing their fellow tribesmen and women. They wanted to drive them out. However, the friars and soldiers caught those responsible for the attack and sent them to the presidio in

Monterey, where they were punished. The Chumash living at the mission helped put out the fires and began rebuilding the mission. The missionaries were determined to stay. They developed a way to make the roofs fire resistant, by covering them with *tejas*, or clay tiles, which could not easily burn. Soon other missions began making tiles for their roofs to prevent fires.

FINISHING THE MISSION

As the mission's neophyte population grew to its peak (832 inhabitants) in the early 1800s, so did the mission complex. Construction ended in 1819, at which time the mission had expanded to contain *monjeríos*, or dormitories, for single neophyte girls and women; soldiers' barracks, storerooms, workrooms, mills, a **granary**, a hospital, and houses for the neophytes. It also included miles of **aqueducts**, which supplied water to the community and gardens; outlying ranchos, or farms; and two *asistencias*, or branch missions. The main church structure was completed in 1793.

To bring water to the missions, soldiers and Native people built aqueducts similar to this one, which was built at Mission San Antonio de Padua.

6
Life at the Mission

For the neophytes, daily life at the mission was more challenging than they expected. The structured lifestyle meant there wasn't much freedom or leisure time, a big change to how the Chumash used to live. The Spanish way of doing things was difficult to get used to for many of the neophytes.

Activities at Mission San Luis Obispo de Tolosa differed little from day to day. Men, women, and children worked very hard, and for long hours, to help the mission function and grow.

DAILY SCHEDULE

Most Alta California missions followed the same daily schedule. The day began around sunrise when the residents were wakened by bells. Bells served the same purpose at every mission: to alert people to a new activity. At Mission San Luis Obispo de Tolosa, the bells were hung from a **belfry** on the second story of the church. In 1820, four new bells arrived from Peru, though two were damaged in the journey and replaced by one bell made in San Francisco. The job of bell ringer was an honor at the mission and usually held by one of the friars. But over time neophytes and other parishioners became involved as well. The ringing of the bells continues to this day.

In the mornings, the mission community gathered and headed to the church for Mass, morning prayers, and church lessons. Afterward came breakfast. The neophytes were served *atole,* a mush made of grain or corn. The residents then went to work.

There were many jobs at the mission for men, women, and children. The Chumash men were responsible for farming, ranching, leather making, ironworking, tanning, carpentry, and construction. The Chumash women cooked the food, made clothing, and created baskets and soap. The Spanish showed them how to weave using European looms. The children helped with other chores and listened to the friars read from the Bible or teach them Spanish. Many missionaries worked side by side with the neophytes.

At Mission San Luis Obispo, the Chumash raised livestock, including sheep, cattle, mules, and horses. They planted wheat, fruit trees, corn, beans, and other vegetables. They also grew grapes to make wine and olives to make olive oil. The Chumash women began using corn and wheat flours instead of acorn flour, though they continued to collect nuts and edible plants, especially in the early years of the mission system before much farming had begun.

After the morning work session ended, the laborers had lunch. They were served *pozole*, a soup made of grain, vegetables, and meat. After lunch they took a *siesta*, or a rest. A short period of work followed in the afternoon. Everyone then reconvened for Mass, dinner, which usually included atole, and prayers. More religious instruction was held during the evenings, as well as Spanish language lessons. Then there was a little time for leisure. The Chumash enjoyed singing and dancing and making their own musical instruments, but while living in the mission they could not practice the traditions or beliefs of their tribes. It was forbidden once a person became a neophyte. Bedtime was at 8 p.m. for the women and children and 9 p.m. for the men.

SPECIAL OCCASIONS

Sometimes the daily routine varied. The Spanish liked to hold *fiestas*, or festivals, honoring various saints, important events in church history, births, and weddings. On these occasions everyone celebrated.

MISSION HARDSHIPS AND TRIUMPHS

Mission life was challenging for the soldiers and friars. Many experienced feelings of isolation being at such a distance from their loved ones and homeland. In addition, they had to adjust to a different environment, climate, and style of living. There were few comforts at the mission, and there were many food shortages. Their living quarters were simple: dirt floors, wooden cots, and scratchy blankets. The food was often bland.

The missionaries performed many duties. They taught the neophytes religion and language; prepared religious lessons; and performed church services, weddings, funerals, and baptisms. Since the missions were under the authority of New Spain's government, the missionaries also had to take care of official business, such as writing yearly reports and keeping records of life at the missions. In 1832, records show that the missions owned 5,422 sheep, 2,500 cattle, 700 horses, and 200 mules. The friars also noted a total of 763 marriages, 2,268 deaths, and 2,644 baptisms over a sixty-year span. Such records are what allow historians today to understand the productivity of each mission.

However, the neophytes' lives were perhaps the most difficult. They left their tribes and families to live a life they thought would be different yet interesting. Yet throughout the mission's existence they worked very hard, earned very little, and dealt with consequences of pain and punishment if a task had not been done properly or if they tried to escape. Although not all missions treated the neophytes poorly, the mission system itself threatened the cultures, traditions, and lifestyles of many tribes.

Over time, conflict at the missions caused many Natives to flee, searching for work as ranch hands in other places.

7
Conflict at the Mission

The trouble that arose between the neophytes and the Spanish friars and soldiers arose for many reasons.

HARDSHIPS

Some of the neophytes that joined Mission San Luis Obispo de Tolosa embraced their new faith of Christianity, but others looked to the Spanish at the mission as providers of food and shelter. The friars set strict rules for the neophytes. No one was allowed to leave without the missionaries' permission. If anyone tried to escape, he or she was captured, returned to the mission, and punished in the presence of the other neophytes. This public treatment was meant to discourage others from trying to leave. However, some neophytes quickly became frustrated and unhappy, and grew even more determined to escape.

Many Spanish soldiers were brutal in their treatment of the neophytes. They were also often lazy, rude, and disorderly. Some were cruel, severely beating and mistreating the neophytes. At that time there was a conflict concerning what group should govern the missions: the friars or the military. Both friars and soldiers were at the missions overseeing daily work. In the 1770s,

Fray Junípero Serra, the head of the missions, challenged the Spanish government on the issue. On one side was the young military commander Pedro Fages, who thought the military should govern the missions. On the other side was Serra, who thought the friars should be placed in charge. In the early 1770s Serra asked the government to remove Fages as military head of Alta California. Serra was successful, though Fages' successor was not much better. Serra obtained a document from the government stating that the missionaries could control the neophytes instead of the military. At the time, this document was considered as the "Native American Bill of Rights," though many soldiers disregarded it and continued the abuse.

The treatment of the neophytes only fueled the anger of the Chumash, who no longer wanted the missionaries on their lands forcing them to adopt a new lifestyle and religion. They attacked Mission San Luis Obispo several times but found their arrows no match for the Spanish guns.

In an attempt to ease relations, beginning in 1780, the missionaries allowed the neophytes to choose one of the converts to become an *alcalde*, or lead neophyte who acted as a go-between for mission and Native relations. Their job was to keep the peace by making sure each side was represented and understood by the other.

NEW DEADLY ILLNESSES

The Spanish arrival in New Spain and eventually in Alta California exposed the population of indigenous people to many European

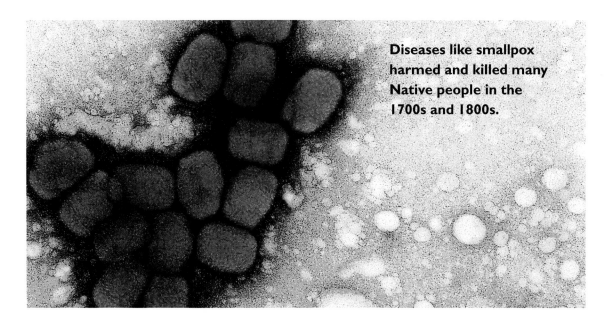

Diseases like smallpox harmed and killed many Native people in the 1700s and 1800s.

diseases unknown to them. Their bodies had not built up immunity to chicken pox, measles, smallpox, or syphilis. Diseases such as these took their toll as epidemics swept through the mission. Many Chumash died.

A NEW FRAY

Despite its problems, Mission San Luis Obispo continued to grow. In 1789, Fray Cavaller died and was buried beneath the floor of the mission's church. He was replaced by Fray Miguel Giribet. Eight years later Fray Luis Antonio Martínez joined Fray Giribet at the mission. Fray Martínez would then spend his entire mission career (1798–1829) at San Luis Obispo. Fray Martínez was a friendly, jolly man who was able to establish good relations with the Chumash. He was also known for his odd antics. According to one story, when a general and his wife visited the mission, Fray Martínez had all the poultry in the barnyard assembled and paraded past the guests. However, he had less success in winning over the military. He often thought soldiers were too lazy, and would easily speak his mind, which eventually led to his deportation to Spain in 1829.

MARTÍNEZ AND THE PIRATES

Perhaps Fray Martínez's most heroic effort took place in 1818 when a **corsair** named Hippolyte de Bouchard and his men arrived off the coast of Monterey. There de Bouchard and his men engaged in a brief skirmish with the presidio, and later came ashore to raid missions Santa Bárbara and San Juan Capistrano. Knowing the missions needed help, Fray Martínez led a group of Chumash from Mission San Luis Obispo to defend the settlements at Santa Barbara and San Juan Capistrano. While the effects of Martínez's actions on de Bouchard and his men are unknown, the pillaging eventually stopped and Hippolyte and his men sailed off.

In 1818, Hippolyte de Bouchard raided the presidio of Monterey. Mission San Luis Obispo trained people for battle against de Bouchard and went to defend other missions from pirate attacks.

8
Secularization

When the Alta California missions originally began, the friars devised a plan for the operation of each mission to be handed over to the neophytes, who by then would be Spanish citizens, after ten years. This process was called **secularization**. However, none of the missions were handed over to the neophytes because the friars never felt they were ready. Then in 1810, the people in New Spain declared war on Spain. They wanted to gain their independence and become their own country. This led to a period of unrest for the missions. Spain had originally sent supplies and money to help the missions, but during the war, these materials were instead going toward the war effort. As a result, money and supplies were not reaching the missions. Despite these obstacles, Mission San Luis Obispo somehow continued to prosper.

SECULARIZATION UNDER MEXICO

In 1821, the people in New Spain gained their independence and named their nation Mexico. Alta California and the missions there now belonged to the Mexican government. Three years later the neophytes at missions Santa Bárbara, La Purísima Concepción, and Santa Inés revolted against the mission system, but the San Luis Obispo Chumash did not. Still, this mission had troubles.

Tensions between Fray Martínez and the military reached a

New Spain (later renamed Mexico) and Spain went to war between 1810 and 1821. Mexico became independent in 1821 and changed the mission system forever.

breaking point in 1829. He was banished from Alta California on charges of treason. In 1832, an earthquake rocked the mission, causing severe damage to the buildings. Then, in 1834, Mexico decided to secularize the missions, but under their own terms.

The Mexican government passed secularization laws in August 1834. These laws took the control of the missions away from the Franciscan friars and gave it to the Mexican government. The government was supposed to redistribute the land to the neophytes and other residents of the mission settlements. Instead, most of the mission property was given as gifts to favored people of influence. Some of the neophytes received small plots of land in and around the mission area. But many left the mission to find work elsewhere or to return to their villages, if they had not been taken over by ranchers or settlers. Some Chumash found jobs as servants and ranch hands on nearby ranches. Others formed small settlements in the outlying areas.

SECULARIZING MISSION SAN LUIS OBISPO

Mission San Luis Obispo was secularized in 1835. In 1845, Governor Pio Pico sold what was left of the mission, except for

In the 1840s, Governor Pio Pico sold much of the lands of Alta California to settlers and government officials.

the church, to Captain John Wilson and his partners, James McKinley and James Scott, for $510. After it was sold, Mission San Luis Obispo gradually fell apart. Several earthquakes during the 1880s left most of the adobe structures in ruins. There were too few neophytes left to repair the structures. Some of the buildings that were still usable were rented out and used as jails, schools, and court-houses. It sat until 1933, when most of the restoration on the mission took place.

Today Mission San Luis Obispo de Tolosa acts as a church and a museum. Its lands have been greatly reduced, and only one square block of the original structure remains.

9
The Mission Alive Today

The mission at San Luis Obispo was returned to the Catholic Church in 1859. Throughout the latter 1800s and early 1900s, various priests began restoring the mission. It wasn't until the 1930s, though, when Fray John Harnett, a parish friar, arrived and began efforts to restore the mission to its eighteenth-century state that it began to resemble its origins.

VISITING THE MISSION

Today Mission San Luis Obispo serves 2,200 families as a church and a community center, as well as a historical site. Visitors come from all over the world to get a glimpse of how the early Californians lived, for unlike most of the other missions of Alta California, San Luis Obispo sits on its original site.

Today only one square block of the original structure remains intact. This structure now serves as a museum decorated with many symbols and drawings done by the Chumash who lived there. Sketches and photographs of the mission line the museum walls. The museum also houses the largest collection of Native American artifacts of all of the California missions. The exhibit cases are filled with grinding stones, tools, and shell ornaments.

Other exhibits include European tools, looms, furniture, and wine vats.

People now know San Luis Obispo as the "City with a Mission." The paintings on the church walls, the baskets still woven the same way they were in mission times, and the unique *teja* roofs of the buildings are all reminders of the Chumash neophytes and the Spanish friars. San Luis Obispo County is filled with vineyards that produce world-famous wines. Mission San Luis Obispo de Tolosa remains a crucial part of the city, as residents still use its church and youth and senior centers on a daily basis. The mission today lets the legacy of its founders and residents live on.

Many walls inside the church are decorated with original artwork drawn by the men and women who lived there.

10
Make Your Own Mission Model

To make your own model of the San Luis Obispo mission, you will need:

- cardboard
- glue
- green construction paper
- mini bells
- pencil
- red beads
- scissors
- tape (or wood glue)
- toilet paper rolls
- toothpicks
- white paint
- wire

DIRECTIONS

Adult supervision is suggested.

Step 1: Glue green construction paper to a large piece of cardboard. This will be the base for your model.

Step 2: To make the church walls, cut three 4" × 8" (10.2 × 20.3 centimeter) pieces of cardboard for the sides and back. Also cut a 4" × 4" (10.2 × 10.2 cm) piece for the roof.

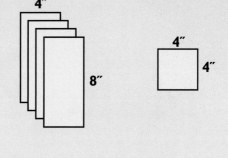

Step 3: Cut a 6" × 11" (15.2 × 27.9 cm) cardboard piece for the church's front. Draw and then cut arched doors and windows. Cut the top so it is triangular.

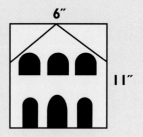

Step 4: Glue a toothpick behind each of the three windows. Use wire to attach a bell to each toothpick. Make a cross out of toothpicks and glue it to the top of the church front.

Step 5: Tape the sides, front, back, and roof of the church together. Paint the church white. Let it dry.

Step 6: Glue the mission church to the base.

Step 7: To make the quadrangle buildings, cut four cardboard pieces measuring 10" × 4" (25.4 × 10.2 cm). Paint them white. Let them dry.

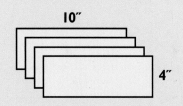

Step 8: Tape the quadrangle walls together in a square and place the square next to the church on the base.

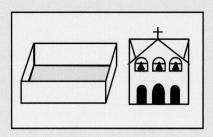

Step 9: Cut two pieces of cardboard measuring 10" × 4" (25.4 × 10.2 cm) for the roofing of the quadrangle buildings.

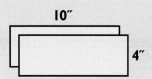

Step 10: Glue red beads to the top of both of the roof pieces. Let them dry.

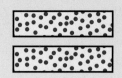

Step 11: Glue one roof panel on top of the back wall of the quadrangle. Place one toilet paper roll under it inside the courtyard for extra support.

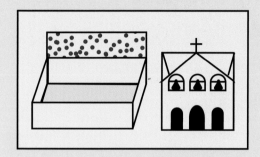

Step 12: Place the second roof panel on top of the front wall of the mission quadrangle. Place the second toilet paper roll under it for extra support.

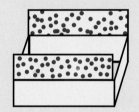

Step 13: Paint both toilet paper rolls and wrap them in fake leaves to make them look like trees in the courtyard.

Step 14: Paint the windows on the outside walls of the quadrangle buildings.

Step 15: Decorate the mission grounds with crosses, trees, and flowers.

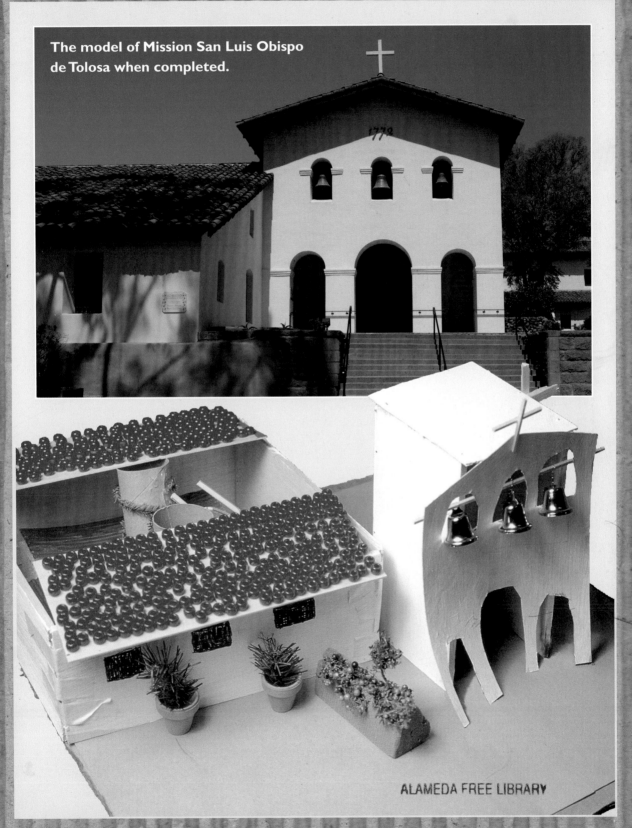

The model of Mission San Luis Obispo de Tolosa when completed.

Key Dates in Mission History

1492	Christopher Columbus reaches the West Indies
1542	Cabrillo's expedition to California
1602	Sebastián Vizcaíno sails to California
1713	Fray Junípero Serra is born
1769	Founding of San Diego de Alcalá
1770	Founding of San Carlos Borroméo del Río Carmelo
1771	Founding of San Antonio de Padua and San Gabriel Arcángel
1772	Founding of San Luis Obispo de Tolosa
1775–76	Founding of San Juan Capistrano
1776	Founding of San Francisco de Asís
1776	Declaration of Independence is signed

1777	Founding of Santa Clara de Asís
1782	Founding of San Buenaventura
1784	Fray Serra dies
1786	Founding of Santa Bárbara
1787	Founding of La Purísima Concepción
1791	Founding of Santa Cruz and Nuestra Señora de la Soledad
1797	Founding of San José, San Juan Bautista, San Miguel Arcángel, and San Fernando Rey de España
1798	Founding of San Luis Rey de Francia
1804	Founding of Santa Inés
1817	Founding of San Rafael Arcángel
1823	Founding of San Francisco Solano
1848	Gold discovered in northern California
1850	California becomes the thirty-first state

Glossary

adobe (uh-DOH-bee)
Sun-dried bricks made of straw, mud, and sometimes manure.

aqueduct (AH-qwuh-dukt)
A type of bridge built to carry water across a valley.

baptism (BAP-tis-um)
A ceremony held when someone accepts the Christian faith.

belfry (bell-free) A bell tower.

Catholicism (ka-THOL-ih-sih-zum) A section of the Christian faith that is led by the Pope and many traditions.

Christian (KRIS-chun)
A person who follows the teachings of Jesus Christ and the Bible.

convert (kun-VURT)
To change from belief in one religion to the belief in another.

corsair (core-SAYR) A type of pirate.

granary (GRAY-nuh-ree)
A windowless building used for storing grain.

mission (MISH-un)
A religious community set up in the early 1600s, late 1700s and mid-1800s that sought to bring Christianity to the Native people of California, as well as and Central and South America.

neophyte (NEE-oh-fyyt)
Native Americans who became Christians and lived at the missions.

nomadic (no-MA-dik)
When a group of people moves from place to place to find new homes and resources to live.

ritual (RIH-choo-wul)
A religious ceremony.

secularization (seh-kyoo-luh-rih-ZAY-shun) When the operation of the mission lands was taken from the friars and turned over to the government.

Pronunciation Guide

alcaldes (ahl-KAHL-des)

asistencias (ah-sis-TEN-see-uhs)

atole (ah-TOH-lay)

La Cañada de los Osos (LAH cahn-YAH-dah DAY LOHS OH-sohs)

fiesta (fee-EHS-tah)

fray (FRAY)

monjeríos (mohn-hay-REE-ohz)

pozole (poh-SOH-lay)

ranchos (RAHN-chohs)

siesta (see-EHS-tah)

tejas (TAY-hahs)

Find Out More

For more information on the missions of California, check out these books and websites.

BOOKS

Brower, Pauline. *Inland Valleys Missions of California.* Minneapolis, MN: Lerner Publishing, 2008.

Gibson, Karen Bush. *Native American History for Kids.* Chicago, IL: Chicago Review Press, 2010.

Padelsky, Londie. *California Missions.* Ketchum, ID: Stoecklein Publishing, 2006.

Rosinsky, Natalie M. *California Ranchos.* Capstone: Edina, MN, 2006.

Weber, Francis J. *Blessed Fray Junípero Serra: An Outstanding California Hero.* Bowling Green, MO: Editions Du Signe, 2008.

WEBSITES

California Missions Foundation

www.californiamissionsfoundation.org

This website offers quick and easy facts for each mission and outlines the group that keeps the missions a part of California's history.

California Missions Resource Center

www.missionscalifornia.com

This is a website that gives great resources on all the California missions.

San Diego History Center

www.sandiegohistory.org

This website offers articles, discussions, and resources about the history of San Diego.

Mission San Luis Obispo de Tolosa

www.missionsanluisobispo.org

This is the official website of Mission San Luis Obispo de Tolosa today.

Mission Tour – History of San Luis Obispo

www.missiontour.org/sanluisobispo/history.htm

This is a website providing a brief history of the mission.

Index